INFUSED!

INFUSED!

70 thirst-quenching, healthy drinks

Angèle Ferreux-Maeght

Photographs by Émilie Guelpa

Smith
Street
Books

CONTENTS

WATER IS LIFE!

Water is the source of life on earth. It's true – we can go several weeks without food, but only a few days without water. It makes up approximately 60% of our body weight and keeps us running smoothly in a multitude of ways. It helps feeds our 50 billion cells, then removes toxins and waste through our kidneys, skin and lungs. It facilitates chemical exchanges within the body which are essential to life. It helps us regulate and maintain our body temperatures, by making us perspire and cool when we are too hot. Water is life!

FINDING THE RIGHT BALANCE

On average, an adult will eliminate about 2.6 litres (88 fl oz) of water every day, through the processes of perspiration and urination. To maintain a good balance between the amount of water that we lose and the amount necessary for the healthy functioning of our bodies, we eat and we drink. Often, we have become aware of the importance of drinking the right amount of water each day from an early age.

WATER, YES, BUT GOOD WATER

We rarely talk about the quality of this precious resource, but it seems fitting to do so here. In many countries, running water is well regulated, but it can still contain traces of bleach, hormones, heavy metals or even pesticides. This is why, when possible, we should try and use filtered water for drinking. Nowadays, there is an abundance of options that offer filtering in your own home. Commercial water filters, such as those offering biodynamic water or reverse osmosis water filtration, to name a couple, are easy to source and use, though can often be expensive.

Alternatively, you can 'clean' your water with natural ingredients.

Two tips for cleaning running water

1 Binchotan charcoal, made from charred oak or bamboo, purifies water by naturally attracting harmful molecules (such as chlorine or mercury). It can also improve water quality by releasing essential minerals such as calcium, magnesium and iron into the water. Water filtered this way is ideal for kitchen use, as well as for preparing infused waters and teas.

2 Ceramic pearls, made of pure clay, are another useful and easy way of cleaning and improving the taste of running water.

What is 'ideal' water?

Ideally, water should be slightly acidic (with a pH below 7), lightly loaded with minerals, and without nitrates.

WATER AND MEALS: FRIENDS OR ENEMIES?

Ideally, we should be drinking small amounts of water throughout the day. When it comes to meals and water, if you feel the need to drink during a meal, go ahead! But it's good to keep in mind that moderation is key. Drinking water with meals can have beneficial effects: it can help dilute the foods that we ingest and facilitate the assimilation and transport of nutrients from food into our blood. When we don't have enough water in our bodies, our blood thickens, making it harder for those precious nutrients to get transported around the body. However, it is best to avoid drinking an excessive amount of water during meals: the presence of a large amount of water in the digestive system decreases the effectiveness of gastric juices, which in turn slows down digestion. If you find you are feeling very thirsty at each meal, try and identify the signs and take action: make it a habit to drink 30 minutes before eating, then 2 hours after.

Note: Drinking water with your meals won't make you gain weight, and drinking water without meals won't make you lose weight ... Sorry!

INFUSED WATERS, OUR BEAUTIFUL ALLIES

Fresh fruit, vegetables, herbs, spices, cereals, good water: with these ingredients we can make wonderful infused waters. In addition to their delicate taste, infused waters are ideal for concentrating the benefits of essential nutrients, especially vitamins.

Unlike fat-soluble vitamins (A, D, E, K, F) that are easily stored within the body, water-soluble vitamins (B, C), found mainly in raw fruits and vegetables, are very difficult to store. In addition, they are often destroyed during cooking – for example, anything above 60°C (140°F) will significantly reduce the benefits of vitamin C! So, finding easy and delicious ways of consuming these vitamins naturally, can be of great benefit to our overall health and well-being.

MIX AND MATCH

Many plants and herbs that we are familiar with, such as thyme, rosemary, verbena, chamomile, mint and lemon balm, are both flavoursome and have beneficial elements when used on their own. But it's also possible to combine plants that have complementary properties in order to tailor something specifically to meet your needs.

Good pairings

• A fruit with a flower;
• a root with a herb;
• a vegetable with a spice.

The possibilities are endless, so give free rein to your spontaneity and personal likes.

When making infusions, use the best quality ingredients you can obtain. Use good quality, organic ingredients when available. Additionally, ingredients that have been through the least amount of processing, for example that have been manually picked, or sun dried, are also preferable.

Note: Hydrosols are distilled floral waters. It is essential that you consult with a medical professional or qualified aromatherapy practitioner before ingesting.

DIFFERENT METHODS

Detox waters

Principle: put cold water with your chosen ingredients, such as a combination of herbs, plants, roots, fruits and cereals, and leave to infuse.

Infusion

Principle: boil water, then pour it over your chosen ingredients, such as a combination of herbs, plants, roots, fruits and cereals, and let steep for a few minutes.

Decoction

Principle: place the plants (stems, thick leaves, bark or roots) in cold water and bring to the boil, covering for 3 to 10 minutes. Leave to infuse off the heat for up to 10 minutes, then strain.

Maceration

Principle: maceration is more suitable for flowers or fragile plants (this is the principle of Bach flowers). Put the plants in cold water and let steep for a few hours to a few days. A maceration can also be done in wine, oil or alcohol.

THE BENEFITS

Water infusions have been used in traditional medicine for millennia. In addition to the sublime aromas they emit, these ancestral techniques capture the water-soluble active ingredients of plants, to our benefit. The active ingredients in plants are downright magical, they work in synergy. Even better, their combination increases their individual powers tenfold. Detox waters and infusions are therefore real treasures to strengthen our bodies on a daily basis.

Herbal teas and infused waters obviously do not replace the fruit and vegetables we need to consume as part of a balanced diet. But they are strong allies to help us better hydrate, revitalise and detox, and turn our backs on sugary drinks. These drinks should not and do not replace any pharmaceuticals or supersede any medical advice you may have been given.

Detox

WATERS

FRUITY AND TANGY

4 CITRUS
LEMON, LIME, ORANGE AND GRAPEFRUIT

boosts immunity, detoxifying

MAKES ABOUT 1.5 LITRES (51 FL OZ/6 CUPS)
INFUSE FOR 15 MINUTES IN THE FRIDGE

1 grapefruit
2 oranges
2 lemons
1 lime
1.5 litres (51 fl oz/6 cups) water
some ice cubes

Wash the citrus fruit and then cut them into rings.
Arrange the slices in a carafe and add the water and ice.
Leave to infuse for 15 minutes in the refrigerator.

Consume in the morning

FRUITY AND TANGY

VITAMIN E
ORANGE AND BLUEBERRY

antioxidant, detoxifying

MAKES ABOUT 1.5 LITRES (51 FL OZ/6 CUPS)
INFUSE FOR 15 MINUTES IN THE FRIDGE

200 g (7 oz) blueberries
4 oranges
2 rosemary sprigs, plus extra to garnish (optional)
1.5 litres (51 fl oz/6 cups) water
some ice cubes

Wash the blueberries, oranges and rosemary. Cut some of the blueberries in half and the oranges into quarters. Place them in a carafe. Add the rosemary sprigs, water and ice. Leave to infuse for 15 minutes in the refrigerator. Garnish the glasses with a small sprig of rosemary.

Consume in the morning

FRUITY AND TANGY

ANTIOXIDANT
RED BERRIES

antioxidant, promotes blood circulation

MAKES ABOUT 1.5 LITRES (51 FL OZ/6 CUPS)
INFUSE FOR UP TO 4 MINUTES AT ROOM TEMPERATURE

125 g (4½ oz) red currants
125 g (4½ oz) raspberries
4 strawberries
some lemon balm leaves
1.5 litres (51 fl oz/6 cups) water
some ice cubes

Gently wash the berries, place them in a bowl, then use a fork to mash
them to a puree. Place the puree in a carafe. Add the ice cubes and
lemon balm leaves, then pour in the water gently. Leave to infuse
for a few minutes at room temperature or drink immediately.

Consume in the afternoon

BITTER AND HERBACEOUS

BITTER
PINK GRAPEFRUIT AND ROSEMARY

antioxidant, good for the heart

MAKES ABOUT 1.5 LITRES (51 FL OZ/6 CUPS)
INFUSE FOR 10 MINUTES TO 2 HOURS IN THE FRIDGE

3 pink grapefruits
3 rosemary sprigs
1.5 litres (51 fl oz/6 cups) water

Wash the grapefruit and the sprigs of rosemary. Cut the
grapefruit into quarters, avoiding the white ribbing of the fruit.
Arrange the quarters in a carafe with the sprigs of rosemary.
Add the water. Leave to infuse for 10 minutes to 2 hours in the
refrigerator, depending on the level of bitterness desired.

Consume before lunch

HERBACEOUS

GREEN
KIWI, CUCUMBER AND CHERVIL

good for the heart and liver

MAKES ABOUT 1.5 LITRES (51 FL OZ/6 CUPS)
INFUSE FOR 20 MINUTES TO 5 HOURS IN THE FRIDGE

1 mini cucumber
1 bunch chervil
2 kiwi fruit
1.5 litres (51 fl oz/6 cups) water
some ice cubes

Wash the cucumber and chervil well. Peel the kiwi fruit, then use a mandolin to cut them into thin slices. Use the mandolin to slice the cucumber lengthways into thin slices. In a large carafe, place the ice cubes, chervil, kiwi and cucumber slices then add the water. Leave to infuse for between 20 minutes and 5 hours in the refrigerator.

Consume in the morning and afternoon

FRUITY

EXOTIC
PINEAPPLE, MANGO, LIME AND BASIL

good for the heart and joints

MAKES ABOUT 1.5 LITRES (51 FL OZ/6 CUPS)
INFUSE FOR 20 MINUTES IN THE FRIDGE

1 pineapple
1 mango
2 limes
8 basil sprigs (preferably micro basil)
1.5 litres (51 fl oz/6 cups) water
some ice cubes

Peel the pineapple, slice it, then cut each slice into quarters. Peel the
mango and cut it lengthways. Wash the limes and basil. Cut each lime
in half lengthways, then into slices. Set aside 4 slices, then cut the
remaining slices into triangles. Gently place the ice cubes, mango, lime,
pineapple and most of the basil in a carafe, then pour in the water.
Garnish the glasses with the remaining basil and place the reserved
slices of lime on the edge of the glass (the smell will prepare the senses
for digestion). Leave to infuse for 20 minutes in the refrigerator.

Consume in the early afternoon

SPICY, FRUITY AND AROMATIC

APPETITE SUPPRESSANT
MELON, THYME AND CHILLI

appetite suppressant,
reduces water retention

MAKES ABOUT 1.5 LITRES (51 FL OZ/6 CUPS)
INFUSE FOR 20 MINUTES AT ROOM TEMPERATURE

1 cantaloupe (rockmelon)
a few thyme sprigs
1 whole dried Espelette pepper or 1 teaspoon
powdered Espelette pepper
1.5 litres (51 fl oz/6 cups) water

To prepare the cantaloupe, cut it in half, scoop out the seeds, then cut each half into quarters. Alternatively you can keep the seeds in for a more rustic appearance, or peel the cantaloupe to increase the melon flavour. Arrange the cantaloupe in a carafe with the other ingredients. Add the water. Leave to infuse for 20 minutes at room temperature.

Consume in the afternoon to avoid cravings

HERBACEOUS AND AROMATIC

HULK
GRAPE, FENNEL AND OREGANO

antioxidant, improves digestion

MAKES ABOUT 1.5 LITRES (51 FL OZ/6 CUPS)
INFUSE FOR 30 MINUTES TO 2 HOURS IN THE FRIDGE

1 bunch oregano
1 large fennel bulb or 3 to 4 small mini fennel bulbs
3 handfuls green grapes
1.5 litres (51 fl oz/6 cups) water

Wash the oregano, fennel and grapes well. Cut the fennel
and the grapes in half (for more flavour). Arrange the
ingredients nicely in a carafe. Add the water. Leave to infuse
for between 30 minutes and 2 hours in the refrigerator.

Consume 30 minutes before meals, ideally

FRESH AND SPICY

DIGEST
APPLE AND CINNAMON

appetite suppressant, improves digestion

MAKES ABOUT 1.5 LITRES (51 FL OZ/6 CUPS)
INFUSE FOR 30 MINUTES AT ROOM TEMPERATURE

3 apples
8 cinnamon sticks or 1 teaspoon ground cinnamon
1.5 litres (51 fl oz/6 cups) water

Wash the apples, then finely slice using a mandolin. Arrange the slices nicely in a carafe. Add the cinnamon, pour in the water and mix gently. Leave to infuse for 30 minutes at room temperature.

Consume 30 minutes before meals

FRUITY

PINK LADY
RASPBERRIES, STRAWBERRIES AND WATERMELON

antioxidant, hydrating

MAKES ABOUT 1.5 LITRES (51 FL OZ/6 CUPS)
INFUSE FOR 1 HOUR TO 3½ HOURS IN THE FRIDGE

200 g (7 oz) raspberries
100 g (3½ oz) strawberries
½ watermelon
1.5 litres (51 fl oz/6 cups) water
some ice cubes

Wash the berries and the skin of the watermelon well. Cut
the watermelon into triangles. Place the watermelon, berries
and ice cubes in a carafe. Add the water. Mix well, then
leave to infuse for at least 1 hour in the refrigerator.

Consume throughout the day

FRUITY AND TANGY

GREEN DRAGON
DRAGON FRUIT, LIME AND LYCHEES

anti-fatigue, anti-stress

MAKES ABOUT 1.5 LITRES (51 FL OZ/6 CUPS)
INFUSE FOR 20 MINUTES TO 1 HOUR IN THE FRIDGE

1 dragon fruit (pitaya)
2 limes
8 lychees
1.5 litres (51 fl oz/6 cups) water
some ice cubes

Wash the dragon fruit and limes. Peel the lychees and keep
them whole. Cut the limes and the dragon fruit into slices. Place
the ice cubes, fruit slices and lychees in a carafe, then pour
in the water. Leave to infuse for 20 minutes or longer in the
refrigerator. The colour will deepen the longer it infuses.

Consume throughout the day

KUMQUAT
KUMQUAT, POMEGRANATE AND BASIL

energising, antioxidant

MAKES ABOUT 1.5 LITRES (51 FL OZ/6 CUPS)
INFUSE FOR 10 MINUTES IN THE FRIDGE

4 basil sprigs
seeds from 1 pomegranate
6 kumquats
1.5 litres (51 fl oz/6 cups) water
some ice cubes

Wash the basil and kumquats. Cut the kumquats into thin slices. Pick the basil leaves. Place the basil, pomegranate seeds and kumquat in a carafe with some ice cubes. Add the water. Leave to infuse for 10 minutes in the refrigerator.

Consume throughout the day up until 4 pm

SPICY AND TANGY

IMMUNITY
LEMON, HONEY AND CLOVES

toning, strengthens the immune system

MAKES ABOUT 1.5 LITRES (51 FL OZ/6 CUPS)
INFUSE FOR 30 MINUTES AT ROOM TEMPERATURE

2 teaspoons honey
2 lemons
15 cloves
1.5 litres (51 fl oz/6 cups) water

Mix the water and honey. Wash the lemons and cut them into slices.
Place the lemon slices in a carafe, add the cloves and pour in the
honey water. Leave to infuse for 30 minutes at room temperature.

Consume 30 minutes before or 2 hours after meals

FLORAL, SPICY AND HERBACEOUS

LOOKING GOOD
TURMERIC, CARROT AND MANDARIN

good for the complexion, antioxidant

MAKES ABOUT 1.5 LITRES (51 FL OZ/6 CUPS)
INFUSE FOR 15 MINUTES TO 2 HOURS IN THE FRIDGE

6 cm (2½ inch) piece turmeric
4 baby carrots or 2 medium-sized carrots
2 mandarins
1.5 litres (51 fl oz/6 cups) water
some ice cubes

Wash the turmeric, carrots and mandarins. Cut the turmeric
and mandarins into slices. Cut the baby carrots in half, or
slice the medium-sized carrots. Place the ice cubes and
other ingredients in a carafe, then pour in the water. Leave
to infuse for at least 15 minutes in the refrigerator.

Consume throughout the day

FLORAL AND FRUITY

PINK KOALA
HIBISCUS, POMEGRANATE AND EUCALYPTUS

purifying, revitalising

MAKES ABOUT 1.5 LITRES (51 FL OZ/6 CUPS)
INFUSE FOR 5 TO 30 MINUTES AT ROOM TEMPERATURE

1 small handful hibiscus flowers
seeds from ½ pomegranate
1 tablespoon eucalyptus or peppermint hydrosol
1.5 litres (51 fl oz/6 cups) water

Place the hibiscus flowers and water into a carafe.
Add the pomegranate seeds and hydrosol. Mix well.
Leave to infuse for 5 to 30 minutes at room temperature.

Consume throughout the day

FLORAL

POTION OF THE AZTECS
CHIA AND AGAVE SYRUP

hydrating, balancing, laxative

MAKES ABOUT 1.5 LITRES (51 FL OZ/6 CUPS)
INFUSE FOR 1 TO 3 HOURS IN THE FRIDGE

1 tablespoon agave syrup
1 tablespoon chia seeds
1 tablespoon geranium or orange blossom hydrosol
1.5 litres (51 fl oz/6 cups) water

Pour the agave syrup and water (room temperature or slightly warm) into a carafe and mix well. Add the chia seeds while stirring with a spoon. Add the geranium hydrosol. Mix everything well. Leave to infuse for at least 1 hour in the refrigerator, until the chia seeds are swelling.

Consume throughout the day, away from meals

FLORAL AND SPICY

JAIPUR
ROSE, CARDAMOM, THYME AND HIBISCUS

good after overindulgence

MAKES ABOUT 1.5 LITRES (51 FL OZ/6 CUPS)
INFUSE FOR 30 MINUTES AT ROOM TEMPERATURE

2 tablespoons cardamom pods
1 small handful dried rose buds, plus extra to garnish
some dried hibiscus flowers, plus extra to garnish
a few thyme sprigs
1 tablespoon agave syrup (optional)
1.5 litres (51 fl oz/6 cups) water

Crush the cardamom pods to release the seeds, then place the seeds and pods into a carafe. Add the rose buds, hibiscus flowers, thyme and water, and leave to infuse for 30 minutes at room temperature. To serve, pour the infusion into glasses and decorate with rose buds and thyme sprigs, and drizzle some agave syrup into each glass, if desired.

Consume throughout the day

VANILLA AND FRUITY

GOOD PEAR
GINGER, PEAR AND VANILLA

anti-fatigue

MAKES ABOUT 1.5 LITRES (51 FL OZ/6 CUPS)
INFUSE FOR A MINIMUM OF 15 MINUTES IN THE FRIDGE

1 pear
1 chunk ginger
2 vanilla beans
1.5 litres (51 fl oz/6 cups) water
some ice cubes

Wash the pear and the ginger. Using a mandolin, cut the ginger into thin strips. Cut the pear into quarters. Split the vanilla beans, scrape out the seeds and add them to 125 ml (4½ fl oz/½ cup) water. Using either a fork or a blender, mix the seeds and water well to loosen the seeds. Place the ice cubes, ginger strips, pear wedges, vanilla beans and vanilla water into a carafe, then add the remaining water. Leave to infuse for at least 15 minutes in the refrigerator. The longer the infusion time, the more aromatic the ginger will become.

Consume throughout the day

FRESH, MINTY AND TANGY

CLASSIC
LEMON, CUCUMBER AND MINT

detoxifying, good for the skin

MAKES ABOUT 1.5 LITRES (51 FL OZ/6 CUPS)
INFUSE FOR 10 MINUTES TO 1 HOUR IN THE FRIDGE

2 lemons
1 mini cucumber
4 mint sprigs
1.5 litres (51 fl oz/6 cups) water
some ice cubes

Wash the cucumber, lemon and mint. Cut the lemons into quarters
and the cucumber into slices. Pick the mint sprigs. Place the ice
cubes, lemons, cucumber and mint into a carafe. Add the water.
Leave to infuse for at least 10 minutes in the refrigerator.

Consume throughout the day

FLORAL AND FRUITY

PURPLE RAIN
LAVENDER, BLACKBERRY AND BLUEBERRY

antioxidant, anti-stress

MAKES ABOUT 1.5 LITRES (51 FL OZ/6 CUPS)
INFUSE FOR 5 MINUTES TO 2 HOURS IN THE FRIDGE

250 g (9 oz) blackberries
250 g (9 oz) blueberries
6 lavender sprigs (fresh or dried)
1.5 litres (51 fl oz/6 cups) water
some crushed ice

Wash the blackberries and blueberries, then cut most of them in half. Rub 3 of the lavender sprigs, releasing the flowers. Place the berries, lavender sprigs and flowers, and crushed ice into a carafe. Add the water. Leave to infuse for 5 minutes to 2 hours in the refrigerator, depending on the taste and colour desired – the floral flavour will deepen the longer it is left to infuse.

Consume in the afternoon or evening

FRUITY AND MINTY

PUNCHY
MINT AND PEACH

energising, refreshing

MAKES ABOUT 1.5 LITRES (51 FL OZ/6 CUPS)
INFUSE FOR 20 MINUTES IN THE FRIDGE

2 peaches
4 mint sprigs
1.5 litres (51 fl oz/6 cups) water
some ice cubes

Wash the peaches and pick the mint sprigs.
Cut the peaches into wedges. In a carafe, arrange the
ice cubes, peach wedges and mint leaves. Add the water.
Leave to infuse for 20 minutes in the refrigerator.

Consume in the afternoon

SWEET AND SLIGHTLY BITTER

BEE POTION
APRICOT, POLLEN AND ROSEMARY

good for the skin, hair and nails

MAKES ABOUT 1.5 LITRES (51 FL OZ/6 CUPS)
INFUSE FOR UP TO 20 MINUTES AT ROOM TEMPERATURE

2 apricots
a few rosemary sprigs
1 teaspoon pollen (ideally fresh pollen)
1.5 litres (51 fl oz/6 cups) water
some ice cubes

Wash and pit the apricots, then cut into them wedges. In a
carafe, arrange the ice cubes and apricot wedges. Add the
water. Serve with a sprig of rosemary and a sprinkle of pollen
in each glass. Drink immediately, to the health of our bees!

Consume 30 minutes before or 2 hours after meals

AROMATIC AND TANGY

ANISEED
FENNEL FLOWER AND LEMON

promotes a balanced nervous system, purifying

MAKES ABOUT 1.5 LITRES (51 FL OZ/6 CUPS)
INFUSE FOR A MINIMUM OF 20 MINUTES IN THE FRIDGE

½ lemon
12 fennel flowers
1.5 litres (51 fl oz/6 cups) water
some ice cubes

Wash the lemon and use a peeler to zest half of it. In a
carafe, arrange the ice cubes, lemon zest and fennel flowers.
Add the water. Leave to infuse for at least 20 minutes in
the refrigerator. The longer the infusion time, the more
pronounced the fluorescent yellow colour will become.

Consume throughout the day

FRUITY AND HERBACEOUS

RIVIERA
FIG AND LEMON THYME

mineralising, energising

MAKES ABOUT 1.5 LITRES (51 FL OZ/6 CUPS)
INFUSE FOR 15 MINUTES IN THE FRIDGE

4 figs
a few lemon thyme sprigs, plus extra to garnish
1.5 litres (51 fl oz/6 cups) water
some ice cubes

Wash the figs and cut into wedges. Wash the lemon thyme then pick the leaves. Place the fig wedges, lemon thyme leaves and ice cubes into a carafe. Add the water. Garnish with extra sprigs of lemon thyme. Leave to infuse for 15 minutes in the refrigerator.

Consume in the afternoon

BITTER

ZOMBIE
CRANBERRIES AND CARNATION

good for the cardiovascular system, antioxidant

MAKES ABOUT 1.5 LITRES (51 FL OZ/6 CUPS)
INFUSE FOR 20 MINUTES IN THE FRIDGE

150 g (5½ oz) cranberries (fresh or dried)
4 edible carnation flowers (preferably organic)
1.5 litres (51 fl oz/6 cups) water
some ice cubes

Wash the cranberries. In a carafe, arrange the carnation
flowers, cranberries and ice cubes. Add the water. Leave
to infuse for 20 minutes in the refrigerator.

Consume throughout the day

ZESTY

LEMON LEMONADE
LEMON, LEMON BALM AND LEMONGRASS

promotes relaxation, vitalising

MAKES ABOUT 1.5 LITRES (51 FL OZ/6 CUPS)
INFUSE FOR 30 MINUTES IN THE FRIDGE

2 lemons
1 lemongrass stalk
2 figs
a few lemon balm sprigs
1.5 litres (51 fl oz/6 cups) water
some ice cubes

Wash the lemons, lemongrass and figs. Cut the lemons into thin
slices and the lemongrass in half, lengthways. Cut the figs into thin
wedges. Wash the lemon balm then pick the leaves. Place the ice cubes,
lemon slices, lemongrass, fig wedges and lemon balm into a carafe.
Add the water. Leave to infuse for 30 minutes in the refrigerator.

Consume throughout the day

FRUITY AND HERBACOUS

SUMMER BEAUTY
PEACH, CUCUMBER FLOWER AND VERBENA

*reduces water retention,
promotes intestinal balance*

**MAKES ABOUT 1.5 LITRES (51 FL OZ/6 CUPS)
INFUSE FOR 20 MINUTES IN THE FRIDGE**

1 peach
1 handful cucumber flowers
1 handful verbena leaves
1.5 litres (51 fl oz/6 cups) water
some ice cubes

Wash the peach and cut it into wedges. Place the ice cubes, peach
wedges, cucumber flowers and verbena leaves into a carafe. Add
the water. Leave to infuse for 20 minutes in the refrigerator.

Consume throughout the day

HERBACEOUS AND PEPPER

GREEN AND GREEN
PEPPERMINT AND CHLOROPHYLL

promotes bowel harmony, vitalising

MAKES ABOUT 1.5 LITRES (51 FL OZ/6 CUPS)
INFUSE FOR 4 MINUTES AT ROOM TEMPERATURE

3 mint sprigs
1 teaspoon chlorophyll or sprouted barley powder
1 tablespoon peppermint hydrosol
1.5 litres (51 fl oz/6 cups) water

Wash and pick the mint. Place the leaves, chlorophyll
or sprouted barley powder and hydrosol into a carafe.
Add the water. Leave to infuse for 4 minutes.

Consume 30 minutes before or 2 hours after meals

FRUITY AND MINTY

PINK PANTHER
BEETROOT, RASPBERRY AND MINT

super mineralising

MAKES ABOUT 1.5 LITRES (51 FL OZ/6 CUPS)
INFUSE FOR 30 MINUTES IN THE FRIDGE

4 mini candy beetroot (beets) or 1 small beetroot
250 g (9 oz) raspberries
a few mint sprigs
1.5 litres (51 fl oz/6 cups) water
some ice cubes

Wash the beetroot, raspberries and mint. Using a mandolin,
cut the beetroot into very thin slices. Pick the mint leaves.
Cut some of the raspberries in half. Place the beetroot slices,
raspberries, mint leaves and ice cubes into a carafe. Add the
water. Leave to infuse for 30 minutes in the refrigerator.

Consume throughout the day

FLORAL

PERFUMED
JASMINE AND OREGANO

promotes intestinal relaxation and balance

MAKES ABOUT 1.5 LITRES (51 FL OZ/6 CUPS)
INFUSE FOR 10 MINUTES IN THE FRIDGE

1 handful jasmine flowers (fresh or dried)
a few oregano sprigs
1.5 litres (51 fl oz/6 cups) water
some ice cubes

Place the ice cubes, jasmine flowers and oregano into a carafe.
Add the water and leave to infuse for 10 minutes in the refrigerator.

Consume throughout the day

TANGY AND FRESH

SUCCULENT
ALOE VERA, LEMON AND BASIL

antioxidant

MAKES ABOUT 1.5 LITRES (51 FL OZ/6 CUPS)
INFUSE FOR 15 MINUTES IN THE FRIDGE

1 large aloe vera leaf or 250 ml (8½ fl oz/1 cup) liquid aloe vera
2 lemons
a few basil leaves
1.5 litres (51 fl oz/6 cups) water
some ice cubes

If using the leaf, slice away the thorny tip and spines on either
side. Allow any sap (a bitter yellow milky-looking liquid) to
drain from the cuts, then rinse. Slice away the skin from the top
and bottom of the leaf, leaving the clear gel. Set aside. Wash
the lemons and cut them into quarters. Place the water and
aloe vera in a carafe and mix. Add the ice cubes, lemon and
basil. Leave to infuse for 15 minutes in the refrigerator.

Consume throughout the day

POWERFUL AND FRUITY

DARLING CHERRY
CHERRY AND BLACK LEMON

reduces water retention, mineralising

MAKES ABOUT 1.5 LITRES (51 FL OZ/6 CUPS)
INFUSE FOR 5 MINUTES IN THE FRIDGE

250 g (9 oz) cherries
3 black lemons (dried limes)
1.5 litres (51 fl oz/6 cups) water
some ice cubes

Wash the cherries and cut them in half. Grate or finely chop the black
lemons. Place the cherries, black lemons and ice cubes into a carafe.
Add the water. Leave to infuse for 5 minutes in the refrigerator.

Consume in the morning or in the afternoon

TANGY, FRUITY AND HERBACEOUS

GRANNY ANNETTE
GRANNY SMITH APPLE AND DILL

regulates the digestive system

MAKES ABOUT 1.5 LITRES (51 FL OZ/6 CUPS)
INFUSE FOR 10 MINUTES IN THE FRIDGE

4 small Granny Smith apples
a few dill sprigs
1.5 litres (51 fl oz/6 cups) water
some ice cubes

Wash the apples and cut them into quarters. Place the ice
cubes, apple wedges and dill sprigs into a carafe. Add the
water. Leave to infuse for 10 minutes in the refrigerator.

Consume throughout the day

ACIDULOUS

CHARCOAL PASSION
CHARCOAL AND PASSIONFRUIT

detoxifying, promotes bowel harmony

MAKES ABOUT 1.5 LITRES (51 FL OZ/6 CUPS)
INFUSE FOR 5 MINUTES IN THE FRIDGE

2 passionfruit
½ teaspoon charcoal powder
3 tablespoons apple cider vinegar
2 tablespoons agave syrup (optional)
1.5 litres (51 fl oz/6 cups) water
some ice cubes

Cut the passionfruit in half and hollow them out. Place the passionfruit
pulp into a carafe along with the charcoal powder and ice cubes.
Add the water, apple cider vinegar and agave syrup (if using) and
mix well. Leave to infuse for 5 minutes in the refrigerator.

Consume 30 minutes before or 2 hours after meals

FRUITY

FLORAL BLUE
CHAMOMILE AND BLUEBERRY

promotes digestion

MAKES ABOUT 1.5 LITRES (51 FL OZ/6 CUPS)
INFUSE FOR 5 MINUTES IN THE FRIDGE

1 handful blueberries
1 tablespoon chamomile flowers (fresh or dried)
2 tablespoons blueberry hydrosol
1.5 litres (51 fl oz/6 cups) water
some ice cubes

Wash the blueberries and halve some of them. Place the chamomile
flowers, hydrosol, blueberries and ice cubes into a carafe and pour
in the water. Leave to infuse for 5 minutes in the refrigerator.

Consume after meals (1 cup)

SWEET AND FLORAL

HABIBI
ORANGE BLOSSOM AND DATES

promotes relaxation, rich in nutrients

MAKES ABOUT 1.5 LITRES (51 FL OZ/6 CUPS)
INFUSE FOR 6 MINUTES IN THE FRIDGE

8 Medjool dates
1 handful orange flowers (fresh or dried)
some orange leaves
2 tablespoons orange blossom hydrosol
1.5 litres (51 fl oz/6 cups) water
some ice cubes

Cut some of the dates in half. Place the ice cubes, orange
flowers and leaves, hydrosol and dates into a carafe. Pour in the
water and leave to infuse for 6 minutes in the refrigerator.

Consume throughout the day

Detox

INFUSIONS

FLORAL AND HERBACEOUS

FLOWERS
HERBAL TEA

*promotes balanced nervous system,
soothes inflammation*

MAKES ABOUT 1.5 LITRES (51 FL OZ/6 CUPS)
INFUSE FOR 5 MINUTES

1 small handful marigold petals (fresh or dried)
1 small handful lavender sprigs
1 small handful carnation flowers
1 small handful sage flowers
1 small handful chamomile flowers
1.5 litres (51 fl oz/6 cups) water

Heat the water. Place all the flowers in a teapot and pour
in the hot water. Leave to infuse for 5 minutes.

Consume in the evening

MEDICINAL
SAVORY, SAGE, THYME AND ROSEMARY

supports the immune system

MAKES ABOUT 1.5 LITRES (51 FL OZ/6 CUPS)
INFUSE FOR 5 MINUTES

1 bunch savory
1 bunch sage
1 bunch thyme
3 rosemary sprigs
1.5 litres (51 fl oz/6 cups) water

Heat the water. Place all the herbs in a teapot and pour
in the hot water. Leave to infuse for 5 minutes.

Consume 30 minutes before or 2 hours after meals

PEPPERY
GINGER, PEPPER AND TURMERIC

*fights against inflammation,
strengthens the immune system*

MAKES ABOUT 1.5 LITRES (51 FL OZ/6 CUPS)
INFUSE FOR 5 MINUTES

6 cm (2½ inch) piece ginger
6 cm (2½ inch) piece turmeric
2 small bunches fresh peppercorns or 1 teaspoon peppercorns
1.5 litres (51 fl oz/6 cups) water

Heat the water. Cut the ginger and turmeric into slices.
Place the ginger, turmeric and peppercorns in a teapot and
pour in the hot water. Leave to infuse for 5 minutes.

Consume 30 minutes before or 2 hours after meals

FLORAL AND HERBACEOUS

BLUE
BLUE PEA FLOWER TEA

promotes relaxation

MAKES ABOUT 1.5 LITRES (51 FL OZ/6 CUPS)
INFUSE FOR 3 MINUTES

1 handful dried butterfly pea flowers
1 rosemary sprig
1.5 litres (51 fl oz/6 cups) water

Heat the water. Place the flowers and rosemary in a teapot
and pour in the hot water. Leave to infuse for 3 minutes.

Consume throughout the day

SWEET PINE
SCOTS PINE AND HONEYCOMB

promotes healing

MAKES ABOUT 1.5 LITRES (51 FL OZ/6 CUPS)
INFUSE FOR 5 MINUTES

2 Scots pine tree sprigs or 1 teaspoon Scots pine hydrosol
1 tablespoon honey, from a honeycomb
1.5 litres (51 fl oz/6 cups) water

Heat the water. Place the Scots pine sprigs or hydrosol
in a teapot and pour in the hot water. Leave to infuse for
5 minutes. Sweeten with honey just before serving.

Consume 30 minutes before or 2 hours after meals

ANISEED

MAMMA
ANISEED, FENNEL AND BLACK CUMIN

galactopoietic (stimulates lactation)

MAKES ABOUT 1.5 LITRES (51 FL OZ/6 CUPS)
INFUSE FOR 3 MINUTES

¼ fennel bulb
1 tablespoon anise seeds (or fenugreek)
12 fennel flowers
1 teaspoon black cumin seeds
1.5 litres (51 fl oz/6 cups) water

Heat the water. Wash and finely cut the fennel and set aside.
Mix the seeds together (coarsely crush them for more flavour).
Place the fennel, fennel flowers and seeds in a teapot and
pour in the hot water. Leave to infuse for 3 minutes.

Tip: you can make this brew in large quantities, filter it
and keep it in the refrigerator for up to a week.

Consume throughout the day

ACIDULOUS

DIGESTIVE
IYOKAN, MILLET AND BARK

promotes digestion, vitalising

MAKES ABOUT 1.5 LITRES (51 FL OZ/6 CUPS)
INFUSE FOR 6 MINUTES

peel of 1 small handful iyokan lemons
1 branch dried millet or 1 tablespoon millet grains
1.5 litres (51 fl oz/6 cups) water

Heat the water. Place the lemon peel and millet in a teapot
and pour in the hot water. Leave to infuse for 6 minutes.

Consume throughout the day

FLORAL AND HERBACEOUS

BEAUTIFUL FIELDS
CHAMOMILE AND YARROW

calming, aids digestion

MAKES ABOUT 1.5 LITRES (51 FL OZ/6 CUPS)
INFUSE FOR 3 MINUTES

2 chamomile sprigs or 1 tablespoon chamomile flowers
1 handful yarrow branches
1.5 litres (51 fl oz/6 cups) water

Heat the water. Place the chamomile and yarrow branches in a
teapot and pour in the hot water. Leave to infuse for 3 minutes.

Consume in the day or evening, after eating

FRUITY AND FLORAL

THE LOVE
ROSES AND LYCHEES

promotes youthful and beautiful skin

MAKES ABOUT 1.5 LITRES (51 FL OZ/6 CUPS)
INFUSE FOR 4 MINUTES

12 lychees
1 teaspoon dried rose buds or fresh, wild, untreated rose petals
1 tablespoon rose hydrosol
1.5 litres (51 fl oz/6 cups) water

Heat the water. Remove the skin from the lychees. Place
the rose buds, lychees and rose hydrosol in a teapot and
pour in the hot water. Leave to infuse for 4 minutes.

Consume throughout the day

HERBACEOUS

CANADIAN
SAVORY AND CRANBERRIES

*promotes health of the kidneys
and urinary system*

**MAKES ABOUT 1.5 LITRES (51 FL OZ/6 CUPS)
INFUSE FOR 5 MINUTES**

3 tablespoons cranberries (fresh or dried)
3 savory sprigs
1.5 litres (51 fl oz/6 cups) water

Heat the water. If using dried cranberries, soak them in hot water for a
few minutes and then drain. Place the cranberries and the savory sprigs
in a teapot and pour in the hot water. Leave to infuse for 5 minutes.

Consume 30 minutes before or 2 hours after meals

FRUITY

HAZEL
PINEAPPLE AND HAZELNUTS

antioxidant, good for the heart

MAKES ABOUT 1.5 LITRES (51 FL OZ/6 CUPS)
INFUSE FOR 4 MINUTES

1 pineapple
1 handful hazelnuts
1.5 litres (51 fl oz/6 cups) water

The day before, prepare the pineapple: peel the pineapple and cut
into thin slices, then dry the slices in the oven at 80°C (175°F)
for 4 hours or in a dehydrator at 40°C (105°F) for 12 hours.

Heat the water. Roast the hazelnuts in the oven at 160°C (320°F)
for 15 minutes. Place the dried pineapple and hazelnuts in a
teapot and pour in the hot water. Leave to infuse for 4 minutes.

Consume in the morning or in the afternoon

FRUITY

WILD
HEATHER AND BLACKBERRY

*reduces water retention,
good for the urinary system*

MAKES ABOUT 1.5 LITRES (51 FL OZ/6 CUPS)
INFUSE FOR 4 MINUTES

125 g (4½ oz) blackberries
1 handful dried heather flowers
1.5 litres (51 fl oz/6 cups) water

The day before, prepare the blackberries: place half of
the blackberries in the oven at 80°C (175°F) for 4 hours
or in a dehydrator at 40°C (105°F) for 12 hours.

Heat the water. Cut the remaining blackberries in half. Place
the heather flowers, dried and fresh blackberries in a teapot
and pour in the hot water. Leave to infuse for 4 minutes.

Consume throughout the day, outside of meals

PEPPERY AND FRUITY

PASSIONATE
PASSIONFRUIT AND PEPPERMINT

promotes digestive balance, energising

MAKES ABOUT 1.5 LITRES (51 FL OZ/6 CUPS)
INFUSE FOR 5 MINUTES

1 peppermint sprig
1 passionfruit
1.5 litres (51 fl oz/6 cups) water

Heat the water. Pick the peppermint leaves. Cut the passionfruit
in half, scoop out the pulp and place it in a teapot, along with the
peppermint leaves. Add the hot water. Leave to infuse for 5 minutes.

Consume throughout the day

SMOKY AND FRUITY

BRETON
SOBACHA AND RED PIPPIN

promotes digestive balance

MAKES ABOUT 1.5 LITRES (51 FL OZ/6 CUPS)
INFUSE FOR 4 MINUTES

2 Red Pippin apples
40 g (1½ oz) sobacha (buckwheat tea) or kacha (roasted buckwheat)
1.5 litres (51 fl oz/6 cups) water

Heat the water. Wash the apples and cut them into wedges.
Place the apple wedges and sobacha or kacha in a teapot and
pour in the hot water. Leave to infuse for 4 minutes.

Consume throughout the day

HERBACEOUS AND FRUITY

FRESH COMPLEXION
STRAWBERRY AND THYME

antioxidant, reduces water retention

MAKES ABOUT 1.5 LITRES (51 FL OZ/6 CUPS)
INFUSE FOR 4 MINUTES

250 g (9 oz) strawberries
a few thyme sprigs
1.5 litres (51 fl oz/6 cups) water

The day before, prepare the strawberries: wash the
strawberries, then cut half into wedges and set aside the
other half. Dry the wedges in the oven at 80°C (175°F) for
4 hours or in a dehydrator at 40°C (105°F) for 12 hours.

Heat the water. Slice the remaining strawberries. Place the
dried and fresh strawberries and the thyme sprigs in a teapot
and pour in the hot water. Leave to infuse for 4 minutes.

Consume throughout the day

HERBACEOUS AND ACIDULOUS

MATCHAMAMA
MATCHA, BERGAMOT AND VANILLA

detoxifying, boosts immunity, anti-stress

MAKES ABOUT 1.5 LITRES (51 FL OZ/6 CUPS)
INFUSE FOR 3 MINUTES

2 vanilla beans
1 teaspoon matcha
3 bergamot oranges
1.5 litres (51 fl oz/6 cups) water

Heat the water. Cut the vanilla beans lengthways, then use a
knife to scrape out the seeds. Place the matcha, vanilla seeds and
250 ml (8½ fl oz/1 cup) of the hot water in a bowl and whisk,
ideally with a matcha whisk, until there are no lumps (this can
also be done in a blender, with warm instead of hot water). Cut
the oranges into slices, place them in a teapot, then pour over
the matcha vanilla water. Leave to infuse for 3 minutes.

Consume throughout the day

FRUITY AND ACIDULOUS

VITAMIN A
LEMON, DRIED APPLE, PINEAPPLE AND ORANGE

promotes blood circulation

MAKES ABOUT 1.5 LITRES (51 FL OZ/6 CUPS)
INFUSE FOR 4 MINUTES

4 slices dried apple
4 slices dried pineapple
4 slices dried orange
zest of ½ lemon
1.5 litres (51 fl oz/6 cups) water

Heat the water. Place all the ingredients in a teapot and
pour in the hot water. Leave to infuse for 4 minutes.

Consume throughout the day

HERBACEOUS

THE CRANBERRIES
MORINGA AND CRANBERRIES

mineralising, antioxidant

MAKES ABOUT 1.5 LITRES (51 FL OZ/6 CUPS)
INFUSE FOR 4 MINUTES

2 tablespoons moringa leaves
2 tablespoons cranberries or goji berries
1.5 litres (51 fl oz/6 cups) water

Heat the water. Place the moringa leaves and the cranberries or goji berries in a teapot and pour in the hot water. Leave to infuse for 4 minutes.

Consume 30 minutes before or 2 hours after meals

COCOA AND FRUITY

KINGSTON
RAW COCOA AND GRATED COCONUT

promotes relaxation,
fights fatigue

MAKES ABOUT 1.5 LITRES (51 FL OZ/6 CUPS)
INFUSE FOR 4 MINUTES

25 g (1 oz) grated coconut
1 teaspoon raw cocoa beans
1.5 litres (51 fl oz/6 cups) water

Heat the water. Roast the grated coconut for 8 minutes in the oven at 160°C (320°F). Crush the cocoa beans using a mortar and pestle or coarsely chop them with a knife. Place the coconut and cocoa beans in a teapot and pour in the hot water. Leave to infuse for 4 minutes.

Consume throughout the day

FRUITY

WARM OAT
OATS, PEARS AND PARSNIPS

detoxifying, good for the skin

MAKES ABOUT 1.5 LITRES (51 FL OZ/6 CUPS)
INFUSE FOR 4 MINUTES

1 parsnip
2 pears
30 g (1 oz/⅓ cup) oats
1.5 litres (51 fl oz/6 cups) water

The day before, prepare the parsnip: peel the parsnip and
cut it into thin slices using a mandolin or a sharp knife.
Dry the parsnip shavings in the oven at 80°C (175°F) for
4 hours or in a dehydrator at 40°C (105°F) for 12 hours.

Heat the water. Wash the pears and cut them into quarters.
Place the parsnip, pear and oats in a teapot and pour
in the hot water. Leave to infuse for 4 minutes.

Consume throughout the day

SPICY AND ACIDULOUS

BALINESE
KAFFIR, LEMON AND GALANGAL

fights against inflammation, vitalising

MAKES ABOUT 1.5 LITRES (51 FL OZ/6 CUPS)
INFUSE FOR 3 MINUTES

1 lemon
6 cm (2½ inch) piece galangal
1 handful kaffir lime leaves
1.5 litres (51 fl oz/6 cups) water

Heat the water. Wash the lemon and cut it into slices. Cut the galangal
lengthways. Place the lemon slices, galangal and kaffir lime leaves in
a teapot and pour in the hot water. Leave to infuse for 3 minutes.

Consume 30 minutes before or 2 hours after meals

SMOKY AND SWEET

BENEVOLENT
PRUNES AND SOBACHA

laxative, mineralising

MAKES ABOUT 1.5 LITRES (51 FL OZ/6 CUPS)
INFUSE FOR 4 MINUTES

6 prunes
40 g (1½ oz) sobacha (buckwheat tea) or kacha (roasted buckwheat)
1.5 litres (51 fl oz/6 cups) water

Heat the water. Place the prunes and buckwheat into a teapot
and pour in the hot water. Leave to infuse for 4 minutes.

Consume 30 minutes before or 2 hours after meals

FRUITY AND SWEET

RED HONEY
RASPBERRIES, HONEY AND DRIED CHAMOMILE

mineralising, soothing

MAKES ABOUT 1.5 LITRES (51 FL OZ/6 CUPS)
INFUSE FOR 4 MINUTES

125 g (4½ oz) raspberries
1 tablespoon dried chamomile
1 tablespoon honey
1.5 litres (51 fl oz/6 cups) water

The day before, prepare the raspberries: dry the
raspberries in the oven at 80°C (175°F) for 4 hours or
in a dehydrator at 40°C (105°F) for 12 hours.

Heat the water. Place the raspberries, chamomile and honey into a
teapot and pour in the hot water. Leave to infuse for 4 minutes.

Consume throughout the day

RELAXATION
LINSEED AND VERBENA

nutritious, promotes digestion and relaxation

MAKES ABOUT 1.5 LITRES (51 FL OZ/6 CUPS)
INFUSE FOR 3 MINUTES

50 g (1¾ oz/⅓ cup) linseed
2 tablespoons verbena hydrosol
1.5 litres (51 fl oz/6 cups) water

Heat the water. Place the linseed and verbena hydrosol in a teapot.
Pour in the hot water and let the seeds swell for 3 minutes. Filter.

Consume throughout the day

SPICY

CHAÏ
6 SPICE AND HONEY

*promotes digestion,
strengthens the immune system*

**MAKES ABOUT 1.5 LITRES (51 FL OZ/6 CUPS)
INFUSE FOR 4 MINUTES**

5 cm (2 in) piece ginger (fresh or dried)
5 black peppercorns
4 cinnamon sticks
1 tablespoon coriander seeds
5 cloves
2 tablespoons star anise
1 tablespoon honey
1.5 litres (51 fl oz/6 cups) water

Heat the water. Place all the ingredients in a large
teapot, and leave to infuse for 4 minutes.
Variation: Add a slice of fresh turmeric and a pinch of nutmeg.

Consume before bedtime (1 cup)

ACIDULOUS AND SWEET

VITALITY
QUINOA AND CANDIED CITRUS

vitalising, promotes pH balance

MAKES ABOUT 1.5 LITRES (51 FL OZ/6 CUPS)
INFUSE FOR 4 MINUTES

2 teaspoons quinoa
5 candied citrus peels (orange, grapefruit, mandarin ...)
1.5 litres (51 fl oz/6 cups) water

Heat the water. Roast the quinoa for 10 minutes in the oven at 180°C (350°F). Place the candied citrus peels and quinoa in a teapot and pour in the hot water. Leave to infuse for 4 minutes.

Consume throughout the day

SWEET AND HERBACEOUS

SESAME
DRIED APRICOTS, ROSEMARY AND BLACK SESAME

vitalising, antioxidant

MAKES ABOUT 1.5 LITRES (51 FL OZ/6 CUPS)
INFUSE FOR 4 MINUTES

1 rosemary sprig
40 g (1½ oz) black sesame seeds
1 handful dried apricots
1.5 litres (51 fl oz/6 cups) water

Heat the water. Place the rosemary, sesame seeds and apricots into
a teapot and pour in the hot water. Leave to infuse for 4 minutes.

Consume throughout the day

FRUITY

BLACK MANGO
BLACK RICE AND MANGO

promotes concentration

MAKES ABOUT 1.5 LITRES (51 FL OZ/6 CUPS)
INFUSE FOR 4 MINUTES

55 g (2 oz) black rice
1 mango
1.5 litres (51 fl oz/6 cups) water

Heat the water. Roast the black rice for 10 minutes in the
oven at 180°C (350°F). Peel the mango and cut it into
slices. Place the black rice and mango into a teapot and
pour in the hot water. Leave to infuse for 4 minutes.

Consume throughout the day

FRUITY AND SPICY

A TASTE OF AUTUMN
APPLE, CINNAMON AND CHESTNUTS

helps digestion

MAKES ABOUT 1.5 LITRES (51 FL OZ/6 CUPS)
INFUSE FOR 5 MINUTES

2 apples
1 handful chestnuts
4 cinnamon sticks
1.5 litres (51 fl oz/6 cups) water

The day before, prepare the dried apple: cut the apple into thin slices
using a mandolin. Dry the apple slices in the oven at 80°C (175°C)
for 4 hours or in the dehydrator at 40°C (105°F) for 12 hours.

Heat the water. Cut the chestnuts into small pieces and roast
them in the oven at 200°C (400°F) for 10 minutes. Place the
dried apple slices, chestnuts and cinnamon sticks into a teapot
and pour in the hot water. Leave to infuse for 5 minutes.

Consume between 2 pm and 5 pm

SPICY

PINK JEWEL
CARDAMOM AND PINK PEPPERCORNS

toning

MAKES ABOUT 1.5 LITRES (51 FL OZ/6 CUPS)
INFUSE FOR 4 MINUTES

1 tablespoon cardamom pods
1 tablespoon pink peppercorns
1.5 litres (51 fl oz/6 cups) water

Heat the water. Place the cardamom pods and pink peppercorns into
a teapot and pour in the hot water. Leave to infuse for 4 minutes.

Consume throughout the day

AROMATIC AND BITTER

GRAPEFRUIT
LICORICE AND GRAPEFRUIT

*boosts immunity,
soothes respiratory tract irritation*

MAKES ABOUT 1.5 LITRES (51 FL OZ/6 CUPS)
INFUSE FOR 4 MINUTES

3 licorice roots
peel of 1 grapefruit
1.5 litres (51 fl oz/6 cups) water

Heat the water. Place the licorice roots and grapefruit peel into a
teapot and pour in the hot water. Leave to infuse for 4 minutes.

Consume throughout the day, without food

PEPPER

KOREAN
GINSENG, DRIED APPLES AND GREEN PEPPER

boosts immunity, toning

MAKES ABOUT 1.5 LITRES (51 FL OZ/6 CUPS)
INFUSE FOR 4 MINUTES

1 green apple
1 bunch green peppercorns
1 or 2 ginseng roots
1.5 litres (51 fl oz/6 cups) water

The day before, prepare the apple: cut the apple into thin slices
using a mandolin. Dry the apple slices in the oven at 80°C (175°C)
for 4 hours or in a dehydrator at 40°C (105°F) for 12 hours.

Heat the water. Place 4 dried apple slices, the green
peppercorns and ginseng roots into a teapot and pour
in the hot water. Leave to infuse for 4 minutes.

Consume in the morning or in the afternoon

FRESH AND FRUITY

STAR STAR
CAPE GOOSEBERRY, STAR FRUIT AND VERBENA

*fights against inflammation,
calming*

MAKES ABOUT 1.5 LITRES (51 FL OZ/6 CUPS)
INFUSE FOR 10 MINUTES

1 star fruit
6–8 cape gooseberries (physalis)
1 handful verbena leaves
1.5 litres (51 fl oz/6 cups) water

Heat the water. Wash the star fruit and cape gooseberries. Cut the
cape gooseberries in half and the star fruit into slices. Place the
star fruit, cape gooseberries and verbena leaves into a teapot
and pour in the hot water. Leave to infuse for 10 minutes.

Consume 30 minutes before or 2 hours after meals

ROASTED AND HERBACEOUS

LADY MORINGA
BROWN RICE AND MORINGA

rich in minerals, proteins and vitamins

MAKES ABOUT 1.5 LITRES (51 FL OZ/6 CUPS)
INFUSE FOR 5 MINUTES

1 handful brown rice
1 tablespoon moringa
1.5 litres (51 fl oz/6 cups) water

Rinse the rice under cold water until the water runs clear. Spread the rice over a baking tray and roast in the oven at 200°C (400°F) for 10 minutes. Heat the water. Place the rice and moringa into a teapot and pour in the hot water. Leave to infuse for 5 minutes.

Consume upon waking

TABLE OF RECIPES

INDEX

Smith Street Books

First published in 2017 by Hachette Livre, Marabout division
58, rue Jean-Bleuzen, 92178 Vanves Cedex, France

This edition published in 2021 by Smith Street Books
Naarm | Melbourne | Australia
smithstreetbooks.com

ISBN: 978-1-92581-165-0

Design and illustrations: Anne-Laure Varoutsikos
Layout: Transparency

For Smith Street Books
Publisher: Paul McNally
Project editor and translation: Aisling Coughlan
Cover design: Murray Batten
Typesetting: Megan Ellis

Printed & bound in China by C&C Offset Printing Co., Ltd.

Book 153
10 9 8 7 6 5 4 3 2 1

Note: The information contained in this book is not medical advice. It is recommended that individuals seek health or medical advice from healthcare or medical professionals.